TO HADISON
HOPE YOU ENJOY
& LOVE MY FOX
NADINE

a Fox Kit's Tale

By
Nadine Lambert

 FriesenPress

One Printers Way
Altona, MB R0G 0B0
Canada

www.friesenpress.com

ISBN
978-1-03-913995-4(Hardcover)
978-1-03-913994-7 (Paperback)
978-1-03-913996-1 (eBook)

1. JUVENILE NONFICTION, ANIMALS, FOXES

Distributed to the trade by The Ingram Book Company

Preface

In early 2021, a fox family moved in next door providing a fabulous mini home safari. ("Safari" really means to travel around, but it is often used when speaking about looking for wild animals.) The red male fox had first been spotted in later December around the winter solstice. He and his black mate visited a few times through January and February.

The den exists under our neighbour's back garden shed. Skunks, possums and racoons, had dug a deep passage under the fence between our yards. The week before we learned the foxes had moved in, I had closed it with a cinder block. I saw the male fox in distress, trying to dig out the block. This would be my opportunity. By moving this block for him, he would know I had seen his need and helped. A silent communication, showing my desire to share in his family. When he came out that evening, the male fox was visibly relieved to find the passage open again. He sniffed the block and looked toward our house. He knew I wanted them to visit and enjoy my yard. It taught me how much everything was thought out, looked for, and remembered. The foxes had definitely scouted possible sites, and considered their pros and cons before choosing this location.

I laughed, clapped and moaned, over their teaching and caring of their one little kit - a smart and inquisitive vixen. About nine weeks after her introduction to the outside world the fox family moved on. At that point the kit was about one third the size of her mother.

My tale begins....

I am a little female fox. I was born around the beginning of April.

This is my Mom, a black female fox. Female foxes are called vixens.

Mom got pregnant around the beginning of February. Approximately seven to eight weeks later I was born in our cozy den. A den is a small cave in the ground, hopefully among tree roots that hold the earth together, and may add a little warmth from the tree itself.

My parents really planned for their new family - me! Usually foxes have five to six babies known as kits. This would have given me lots of playmates, but I energetically entered the world outside as their only kit.

Initially a fine gray wool-like fuzz grew thickly all over me. For the first two to three weeks I couldn't control my body temperature. During that time my Mom never left me, keeping me warm by tucking me in close to her. She had to make sure I wouldn't freeze. I couldn't hear or see anything either during those first two weeks. My eyes were still closed, and my ears were blocked. When my eyes finally opened, they were blue. It was another two to three weeks before they started to change to the amber colour my parents have.

Dad is a handsome red fox. Male foxes are called dogs. Dad looks like he is wearing long black opera gloves on his legs and feet, with white tips on his toes. His tail is thick and lush. Foxes are named for their thick haired tails. The scientific name for a red fox is *Vulpes vulpes.*

I didn't know it yet, but I would soon learn that Dad is responsible for the safety and security of our family. He is the alpha, which means that he is the boss, the one most in charge. He watches and listens to everything happening in the world around us. Dad makes sure it is safe for us to concentrate on other things, like playing and eating. His main job is to be constantly on guard.

Over several days, Dad had carefully watched the humans who lived in the houses around our den. He decided this would be a safe place for his family. The humans watched and didn't chase him away. They stayed inside their homes, or they were busy elsewhere.

Both my parents started searching for this perfect accommodation in December. Early one February morning, Mom approved the birthing den by crouching low, rolling onto her back, and touching her nose with Dad's. They had found their new underground home, complete with kit-proof amenities.

The den was being used by a skunk when my parents found it. When Mom finally needed it, she guided the skunk out in a playful manner. Of all the possible homes, our den had the most to offer. This was my hiding place for about ten weeks.

Dad dug the den deeper creating a spray of soil, which made a mound that somewhat hid the opening from the outside. Being deep also kept the den warmer.

My parents had a list of necessities for our home. The den and surrounding area had to keep me safe, contained, and exercised. Several shed roofs provided a great vantage point to observe the surrounding yards, the humans, their doings, and possible intrusion. There were raised planters and wood piles, where Dad warmed in the morning sun after a night of hunting - or to get away from my constant demands.

Outside the den, my home yard was flat and open. A tunnel existed into the neighbouring yard. This was a perfect exercise area, a place for me to build my muscles and skills. It had so many levels for jumping, climbing, hiding, and resting with a view. Both yards had fences all around, blocking my way to the street.

I was just three weeks old, when it was finally time to be introduced to the outside world. There were so many new sights, sounds, smells, and adventures to experience. My parents stayed very close and watchful that first outing.

Initially, I was never alone. The world was mine to explore, as long as I did as my parents told me. I learned quickly, including to appreciate my place in the family.

Both Mom and Dad played with me, encouraged me, and watched over me. Mom provoked teasing and tussling with me, while Dad was always foremost on guard duty. The moment he heard something different he would stop everything and listen. I was taught to immediately dive into the den for protection, while Dad investigated. He would jump to the top of the fence, and then stride up a shed roof to observe the surrounding world. When he was satisfied that no harm would come to us, I was allowed to come back out.

I was so cute! I had thick fuzz to keep me warm. I had a short turned-up nose and almost full-sized paws. I even had a white tip on the end of my tail, just like my Mom.

At one month old, red and white patches started appearing on my face. My ears stood erect, and my nose slowly started to lengthen.

I was still drinking my mom's milk and would enjoy that for another three to four weeks, but Dad had plans to introduce meat into my meals.

When I open my mouth very wide it is a greeting, a display of friendship, an invitation to play. Sometimes my parents made me ask over and over before the fun began.

They work so closely as a loving couple, often touching their noses together in a fox kiss.

In the beginning, either Mom or Dad would go out at night, returning as the warming sun rose and brought a new day. One night both of them left. I woke up alone and decided to look for them. I was curious to know what took them into this nighttime world. They had shown me where I could crawl under the fence to expand my search. This was what I did.

When Mom came home I wasn't there. I was hiding in the adjoining yard under the bench. I was safe, but she was really annoyed! She pounded on me with both her front legs. She drilled home that I was not smart enough, or big enough to be out on my own yet. I didn't know the dangers. There were things out there that were bigger and quicker than me. Things that would love to take and eat a little kit.

That was my first really important lesson. When there are strange sounds and activity, I am to run into the den. I would be told when it was safe to come out.

There were many busy things going on. It was Spring and many animals have babies to feed. For some, a little kit can be a tasty morsel. Dad wasn't always there to help watch. Mom kept pacing that day, and was super protective.

I really learned that lesson.

Three times later that day, she tried to get me to leave my home yard. I remembered her thrashing, and stayed by the den. The humans were big, and this lesson had made me afraid of them also.

That evening, I finally realized Mom was going to be with me to investigate the second yard. She would check an area while I watched, then I would be allowed to explore it by myself. She started down the steps, peering through the glass basement doors.

Next she went up and circled the porch twice. There was a human standing just inside the glass doors. The human crouched down, becoming smaller. Mom visibly let out a huge sigh of relief. She knew I wouldn't be hurt.

Mom stood at the bottom of the porch stairs, allowing me controlled freedom to examine everything. There was more to see behind the glass doors. I went to look again. Mom patiently watched and waited.

There were red tulips and yellow daffodils. When I pressed my nose against a tulip, it would bend backwards. I was stronger than this red flower. I pulled away to look and it bounced back, hitting my nose. The indignity! I pressed again. This time when I pulled back I was ready for it. Vengeance! I nipped a petal off. I would teach it, and shook it back and forth.

I managed to teach several tulips that same lesson the next morning. There were red petals scattered all over.

I snapped at a daffodil leaf, but it didn't taste very good.

I needed more to play with. I found the end of a rope around a bush. I could tug and tug on this, and it wouldn't give an inch. It wasn't as sharp as biting the stems of the rose bush.

It was much more fun to leap on Mom. She would chase me and give me loving nips.

Since I didn't have any brothers or sisters, I tormented both my parents, demanding their attention. I jumped on them, and we would tumble and struggle. They would pin me down. They were always so careful to hold me with the sides of their legs, never their claws. I would catch their tail or a leg, and loved nipping just in front of one of their ears.

As I got older, I would stand on my hind legs and try to push my opponent over. I never won against my parents, so took huge delight making unguarded attacks from behind.

My favourite play was chasing around the yard. We tore through the gardens, along the curbs, around planters, down through the lower garden, and up and around again. But I had an advantage. I was so small I could run through the metal fence. Mom couldn't. I would jump and turn; we stared at each other. I was sure she was proud of my quick thinking. She jumped sideways along the fence facing me, which provoked more chasing.

Some of the fence ran right beside the high curbing. Mom couldn't fit in here. She would walk along the top of the curb, following me with her nose. For me climbing out was still a challenge.

Mom and Dad taught me how to be part of fox society. We groomed each other, which reinforced closeness and social bonds. It provided care and pleasure to us.

I know to put my ears back and down, to indicate submission. "Submission" means, I will obey and do what my parents decide is best. I will not challenge what they demand.

I had to learn my place in the family.

Dad is the alpha, the leader. He has knowledge, experience, and cunning. He takes charge of our well-being. Mom is the beta, the second in command. She also listens to, and supports Dad's decisions.

Submissive body language is important from a very early age. Dad walks tall to show authority. I learn the respectful submissive crouch, remaining low to the ground, with my head extended, ears flat, eyes narrowed, and gaze directed away from Dad or Mom. Dad now stares directly at me. I extend my nose to touch his. As I learn Mom stands beside me, watching closely that I do everything right.

Mom sometimes even rolls over, exposing her soft vulnerable stomach to Dad. She trusts him, and lets him think he is stronger than her.

I have watched Mom. She is sly and cunning. Cunning like a fox.

I had blissfully had the run of my protected world for three weeks. Then my parents decided Mom needed to leave us for a couple of days. I was to learn another lesson. With my main playmate gone I sniffed the yard lethargically.

Dad brought me meat. Something new to play with. My teeth were small, and my mouth wasn't big or strong enough yet to rip through the skin. I couldn't bite this. Dad's jaws were strong. He could. I missed Mom and was hungry for her milk.

The next night as I was wandering in my exercise yard, Mom came bounding between the houses. She ran over the shed roof, jumping along the fence top, down to the wood pile and across the garden. She was home. We raced to each other in an excited greeting.

My teeth were growing and soon Mom wouldn't be able to feed me anymore. My fat round tummy was going to thin out.

One or both of my parents would go out at night and bring back various treats. The yard became a buffet of squirrel, rat, vole, rabbit, baby bird and mouse parts. One night they even brought home a huge pig's thigh bone. We left rabbit tails, squirrel tails, and a few of the longer bird feathers. Mostly we cleaned up everything, devouring bone, fur, and all.

I fight fiercely to keep the gifts of food. If I had siblings, I would have slammed aggressively into them sideways, using my whole body. I tried this against Dad's side while he was carrying some food I wanted. I just slid between his long legs, collapsing right under his tummy.

Since I only had my parents, I had to teach them that once they gave me a nugget, it was mine to do with as I wanted.

Dad took charge of teaching me to cache what I couldn't eat. "Caching" means to hide in a secure place for future use. He would chomp rabbits or squirrels in half, leaving me half, and caching the rest for later consumption. If he was home before I got up, he would dig a hole and hide my new food in it. He knew searching for, and finding the cache, would help me learn and understand what I needed to do, to protect what I would provide for myself in the future.

First I had to know how to dig. Then I had to learn to use my nose to cover my stash with leaves. Strong scents are needed to help cover the dead animal smell.

Dad would send me off with a piece to hide. He would turn his back, pretending to be disinterested. I would bound around, carefully picking a place to dig my hole. Holes need to be deep enough, and somewhere they are not easily seen, or smelt. When I had finished, Dad would dutifully look and sniff through the garden, finally picking up the treat.

I would try again and again over a few days. There was so much to know about storing your food!

In a couple of weeks we had so much carrion around the place. "Carrion" is dead animal meat. I soon learned it was just as valuable to feed other animal's hungry tummies as it was for little kits.

The red-tailed hawk would sit above us, watching every move. He had a family to feed as well.

His presence scared the song birds nesting close by. All the birds would start to squawk at once. The robins, cardinals, and crows took turns dive-booming the hawk. I would sit and watch the commotion.

I was getting better at protecting my food. I now knew to cache it near flowers, or places with a stronger odour.

I left a squirrel head in the garden for several days. I eventually discovered it in the yard waste bin. Flipping it in the air, I gave my mom a tilt of my head, as if to say, "You call this caching?"

One afternoon my parents were visibly cooking up a plan. They were standing looking at each other from opposite ends of the yard. Every now and then Mom would bob her head, "OK, I agree".

It was time for me to learn to hide me.

Dad knew the best way to keep safe when outside was to always hide in the shadows. He often snoozed hidden in the back corner, curled under the cedar tree. If the human came out he would lurch awake, immediately scrambling and scratching the fence as he jumped up. The human would also jump with surprise, and everything would come to a standstill.

Mom would remain in the yard when the human came out to hang things on a line across the grass. Mom would stand and watch, sending subtle messages; like cracking rabbit bones between her teeth.

She taught me the first steps of hiding: first find something fairly solid and larger than you are. She leapt into the middle of the irises, breaking and bending many. I leapt on her. This was fun! We tussled right there, breaking more flower stems. She looked back at the human, so proud to share this lesson and my progress.

That afternoon, we found the irises blocked with tomato cages. Message sent and received.

It was too late for a large bunch of daffodils. What a great cool place for a little kit like me to fall into sideways.

Dad loved to curl up in the tiger lilies at the back fence. Deeper sleep happened in the raised planter. It took a couple of weeks, but I grew strong enough to jump onto the bench, then up to the planter - another place I could join them.

I dug a super deep hole in the home yard. My parents told me there was food in the ground. I needed to learn to listen for things travelling below the surface. Worms, beetles, ants, and larva will help to feed me. Most important were mice, which we can hear squeak up to one hundred feet away.

One day Mom was down past her shoulders in my hole. I stealthily circled behind and leapt on her back. We were both surprised and jumped high into the air. Rather than being upset, she played hard with me. Later I put my head in the hole. Had she found something?

Dad would lick up little insects from the pavement. Here was another place to listen and search for food. I too found bugs hiding between the stones, and could lick up a small bite of protein.

Dad always encouraged me.

When I pawed at the earth, I would sometimes hear movement. I learned I could hear more if I put my nose close to the ground and jumped with my hind legs. This helped to scare the critters below into moving. Often I would jump several times, listening and watching. This game was good to practice, especially as the deep hole where I scared Mom had been filled in.

I was still small and didn't have much weight. Foxes weigh one third as much as a dog of the same size.

It had only been two months since I was born, but I was changing shape. My chest narrowed, and my legs grew longer and stronger. My paws didn't look as big anymore. My eyes were now amber. I was starting to get guard hair through my fluff. The colouring on my face matches my Mom's, with a black mask across my eyes. I have a narrow bib across my chest. I will be more black, like Mom. By the time I am six to seven months old, I will be as big as she is!

My home was changing also. The humans have migrated outside. They were exceptionally busy last May weekend. There were all sorts of very loud bangs, with sparkles in the air. So much noise and activity!

I felt frightened and stayed deep in my den. Mom and Dad spent nearly all their time jumping from shed roof, to fence, to shed roof, watching all that was going on. It was a very distressing few days.

Now we play more just before dusk and dawn. We hide during the day.

I have learned an awful lot since the morning hiding under the bench. I can now run like the wind, whizzing past Dad, while finding a short-cut to catch Mom. I can only jump up about two feet, but down about three feet. It is scary. I hesitate at first, but I am brave.

Today is the last Saturday in May. We need to leave this place. My parents are eager to relocate us into the ravine close by. No more dens unless the weather is bad. We will live and sleep, hiding in the open.

"Tonight" Mom whispers in my ear. I will finally be going with them. I will learn to hunt. I am so excited! I race back to the den to rest and prepare for the departure.

We clean up the cached food, leaving behind only a few tails of various sorts. During the night Mom and I slip into my parents' forbidden world.

Tomorrow morning Dad will slip out of this sanctuary for the last time, taking one last look around. Passing under the window with the human, he pauses, looking up to acknowledge with a final nod.

Fox Fact

Vulpes vulpes – this is the scientific name for the red fox.

Centuries ago, when people started naming plants and animals, Latin was the most widely used language by those who were well-educated. So as not to create any confusion, Latin remains the language to identify every plant and animal.

There are seven areas that make up the identification of animals.

First is the Kingdom, *Animalia* - Latin for Animal

The sixth and seventh areas of identification make up the Latin name used when identifying a specific type of animal. In this tale we are identifying a red fox.

Each name for each species is two parts.

The first part of the name is the genus to which the animal belongs. The genus is a class or group of animals that have common characteristics. The genus name is always capitalized. In this case "*Vulpes*" refers to the entire fox family.

The second part of the name is the species within the genus. In this case, "*vulpes*" identifies the red fox, making its full Latin name *Vulpes vulpes*.

The Arctic fox is *Vulpes lagopus*.

About the Author

As more and more wildlife make their way into human habitat, Nadine found her home had been chosen as a safe space for a fox family to welcome their new kit. What grew from there was a relationship of trust and respect. Nadine observed this young family, making changes in the yard when they weren't there. They in turn, shared their kit's development with her. The foxes allowed Nadine to photograph them as they taught their little one techniques of hunting, socializing and survival. They went out of their way to provide her with a greater understanding of their needs—lessons Nadine is now sharing with young readers through her writing and photography.

Now retired, Nadine spends much of her time observing and photographing wildlife. During her travels, she has had many amazing and unique animal interactions, allowing her to appreciate this intimate opportunity depicted here in her debut publication, *A Fox Kit's Tale*.

CPSIA information can be obtained
at www.ICGtesting.com
Printed in the USA
BVHW020449280822
645560BV00002B/17

9 781039 139954